A Whole World of Cooking

A WHOLE WORLD OF COOKING

by Rebecca Shapiro

Illustrated by the author

BOSTON   LITTLE, BROWN AND COMPANY   TORONTO

In Memory of
the Legacy
of
My Father

FIRST EDITION

T 04/72

Published simultaneously in Canada
by Little, Brown & Company (Canada) Limited

PRINTED IN THE UNITED STATES OF AMERICA

Contents

Introduction

COME WITH ME on a cooking tour around the world. You will be delighted with the marvelous adventure each recipe provides, as you look in on other people, their lands and the way they live.

Ride with the Texas cowboy for a bowl of Chili Con Carne. Go over the Andes for Peruvian Pie of the Sierra. Swim a fjord for a Norwegian Sunday Breakfast. Climb the high Himalayas for Tibetan Chapali.

All these pleasures are yours, all the recipes made from everyday and easily available ingredients. But it is the way the foods are prepared, from what grows and what is available, that make them "specialties" of their particular part of the world.

You will discover many fascinating facts. The Chileans cook grated corn in a wrapping of corn leaves for a dish called Humitas. An ancient Indian and very practical custom, the leaves are used as we would use aluminum foil. The early cowboys of Uruguay (and Argentina, Chile and Brazil) barbecued whole sides of cattle. Today the barbecue (of grilled steaks and assorted meat cuts), called parrillada, is part of the everyday life in the cities of Uruguay.

Most important, you will be eating good food, simply made.

As you begin to cook your way around the world, read each recipe through a few times and visualize it step by step. Line up your ingredients and utensils. Take care of small tasks, such as greasing a pan. Use your imagination, cook unhurriedly and with care. Stay with it. And enjoy yourself; you are creating a precious dish.

I wish to thank the many kind and generous people in the United States, South America and Europe for sharing their recipes and interesting bits of information with me. Thanks to friends and family for listening and tasting, and to the University of Pennsylvania for being there and representing for me a lookout on the world. Special thanks to Señor Edmundo Novoa for sharing good food and good humor. And for his standard remark, which may very well become yours, "The best food we eat at home."

R. S.

Texas Chili Con Carne

BRAVE free spirit, lonely rider, folk hero of the West, the Texas cowboy warms his "innards" with a bowl of hot chili. For this Mexican-American dish, tough meat is cut into little pieces, to be eaten by a tougher American cowboy.

1½ tablespoons salad oil	1 tablespoon flour
1 onion, chopped	½ cup canned tomatoes,
1 tablespoon chili powder	chopped
2 cloves garlic, cut up fine	1 cup canned kidney
1 pound lean beef, cut	beans
into ¼-inch cubes	¼ teaspoon salt

Heat the oil in a saucepan. Add the onion, chili powder, garlic and beef. Cook over high heat, stirring constantly until meat is browned on all sides. Turn to low heat, add the flour, stir until well blended. Add the tomatoes, cover and cook for 1 hour. Rinse the beans in cold running water. Drain. Add the beans and salt to the meat mixture. Cover and cook for 20 minutes.

This tastes better on the second day. *Serves 4.*

Navajo Fry Bread

ALONG the wind-swept craggy red cliffs of the Arizona wild lands, the Navajo brings his sheep back to the corral at the end of the day. In the coziness of the hogan, little fry breads are made to be dipped in honey.

1 cup flour
1 teaspoon baking powder
½ teaspoon salt
½ cup lukewarm water

8 to 10 tablespoons solid
shortening for frying
Honey or jam

Use a sieve to sift the flour, baking powder and salt together into a bowl. Stir in the water, then mix with your fingers and knead lightly by digging in with the heel of your hand, making a soft dough. Dust with flour if the dough is sticky. Roll out dough ¼-inch thick on a lightly floured surface. Cut into squares, just under 2 inches.

Melt the shortening in a sturdy saucepan. When hot and almost smoking, quickly fry 2 to 3 squares of dough at a time; they will puff up. Brown one side, then the other. Drain on absorbent paper. Serve hot with honey or jam on the side. *Makes 24 fry breads.*

Wyoming Glazed Nuts

FROM this big and sprawling land, glazed nuts are a bit of Wyoming hospitality that satisfies everyone. Once you have eaten these tasty morsels, you will hardly stop crunching away. A small jar of glazed nuts makes a nice gift.

1½ cups mixed nuts,   *¼ cup water*
salted or unsalted   *1 teaspoon vanilla*
½ cup sugar   *½ teaspoon cinnamon*

Heat the nuts in a skillet over low heat, mixing gently with a spoon. This takes only a few minutes. Allow nuts to remain in skillet.

Cook the sugar and water in a saucepan over medium heat to the soft-ball stage. (Test by dropping a little syrup into a cup of cold water; it should drop as a thread and dissolve as it reaches bottom.) Remove from heat. Add the vanilla and cinnamon, beat with a fork for 6 to 8 minutes until creamy. Add the nuts. Mix and beat for 3 minutes until all the creamy syrup is mixed in with the nuts. Turn out on a large plate and allow to cool.

Raspberry Apples

WHAT is the state of apples in the state of Washington? They are raspberried, strawberried and cherried. Not a bad way to treat apples, especially for dessert.

3 large apples
1 3-ounce package raspberry,
  strawberry or cherry gelatin
1 cup boiling water

Wash and core the apples. (Use a small knife to cut through from one end to the other, removing centers.) Pare the apples one-third from the top. Place in a medium-sized saucepan.

Empty the gelatin powder into a mixing bowl. Add the boiling water, stir until dissolved. Pour liquid over apples. Simmer over low heat until apples are tender, about 20 minutes. Allow to cool. Serve the apples in individual dessert dishes, spoon the syrup into each dish. *Serves 3*.

Cornmeal Crisps

WE CAN THANK the Indians for corn and cornmeal. And the prairie lands of Iowa and Illinois for providing us with corn. Now we have cornmeal crisps, thin rounds of crackers that can be topped with any meat, cheese or salad spread.

½ cup cornmeal	2 tablespoons butter, melted
¼ cup flour	4 tablespoons milk
¼ teaspoon salt	

Sift together the cornmeal, flour and salt. Add the melted butter and milk. Stir and knead the dough for 2 minutes. Divide into 12 balls. On a lightly floured surface and using a floured rolling pin (or a large smooth-surfaced empty jar) roll each ball into 4½-inch rounds. Lift with a spatula and place on an ungreased baking sheet. Bake in a preheated 375-degree oven for 12 to 15 minutes or until lightly browned around the edges. *Makes 12 cornmeal crisps.*

New England Sour Milk Pie

IN THE OLD New England farmhouse, milk that went sour was put to use by the thrifty housewife. Made into sour milk pie, it was sometimes served at breakfast, giving the hardworking farmer a good start for the day.

To make sour milk, pour 1 cup of milk into a glass and let it stand at room temperature for 24 hours. Overnight is not enough.

PASTRY FOR 9-INCH PIE CRUST

1 cup flour	*4 tablespoons butter*
½ teaspoon salt	*3½ tablespoons iced water*

Sift together the flour and salt. Use a fork to cut the butter into the flour, making a crumbly mixture. Add the water, stir, then press the pastry dough together. Roll out on a lightly floured surface until it is slightly larger than the pie plate. Fold pastry in half, place it on the pie plate, unfold, covering the entire surface. Make a high fluted edge from the overlapping dough.

FILLING

⅔ cup sugar	*2 egg yolks*
2 tablespoons flour	*1 cup sour milk*
2½ tablespoons butter	*2 egg whites*

To separate the egg yolk from the egg white, crack the center of the egg against the rim of a bowl. Hold the egg over the bowl, break the top half of the shell away from the bottom half, allowing the egg white to run into the bowl and

6

the egg yolk to remain "cradled" in the bottom half of the
shell. Empty egg yolk into another bowl.

To make the filling, mix the sugar, flour and butter in a
deep bowl. Add the egg yolks, beat until smooth. Stir in the
sour milk. Beat the egg whites (add a pinch of salt) until
foamy. Fold into the sour milk mixture, then pour it into
the unbaked pastry shell. Bake in a preheated 375-degree
oven for 40 minutes or until lightly golden and firm in the
center.

Liver Spread

You'll want to have a party just to serve liver spread. The Central Europeans who settled in this country had a way of making ordinary liver into a delicacy that has become a great favorite.

1 hard-cooked egg   *½ pound beef liver*
1½ tablespoons salad oil   *Mayonnaise*
1 medium onion, sliced

To hard-cook the egg, cook egg in gently boiling water for 15 minutes. Put into cold water, remove shell.

Heat the oil in a skillet until it is hot but not smoking and brown the onion. Remove onion to a side dish. Pat the liver dry, fry it on both sides until redness disappears. In a wooden chopping bowl chop the liver, onion and hard-cooked egg to a smooth paste. (Or put them through a meat grinder.) Add mayonnaise, about 1 tablespoon, to moisten.

May be served on Cornmeal Crisps or on toasted bread rounds cut from a long Italian-style roll. *Serves 3.*

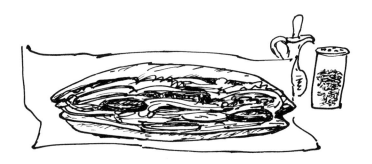

Hoagie, Hero, Submarine or Poor Boy
(*A movable sandwich feast*)

THE HOAGIE is a long bread sandwich known by different names in different areas. The fillings vary. Most satisfying of sandwiches, it is good at any time. Wrap it up and take it with you; it travels well. This is the Philadelphia version.

A loaf of good Italian or French bread (about 15 inches long)
Smoked meat: capocolla (Italian salami), prosciutto (Italian ham)
Cheese: provolone
Tomato, thinly sliced
Onion, thinly sliced into rings, then cut halfway, making strips
Lettuce, chopped
Oregano
Red pepper (optional)
Olive oil

Slit the bread lengthwise. Remove some of the soft bread from the top half. Arrange slices of the meat along the fold of the bread. Layer the cheese, tomato, onion strips and lettuce. Add a dusting of oregano and red pepper. Sprinkle lightly with olive oil. Close the sandwich, press down hard and cut in half. *Serves 2.*

Pennsylvania Dutch Shredded Carrot Mold

YOU DON'T have to go to Paradise or Bird-in-Hand, Pennsylvania, for shredded carrot mold. But you can have a bit of paradise when you serve this crunchy salad mold with any meat or fish.

2 large carrots	*1 cup boiling water*
1 3-ounce package	*1 cup cold water*
pineapple gelatin	

Shred the carrots into little narrow strips on a shredder.

In a deep mixing bowl dissolve the gelatin in the boiling water. Add the cold water, stir, add the shredded carrots and mix well.

Pour the mixture into a glass serving dish. Chill in the refrigerator until firm. Cut into squares and serve. *Serves 6.*

Southern Sweet Potato Pudding

ALTHOUGH boiled sweet potatoes are good, in the South they are perked up with cinnamon and lemon flavoring and glamorized with a marshmallow topping. A sweet potato dish has become almost a "must" at Thanksgiving.

3 medium sweet potatoes	*1 egg, beaten*
(about 1¼ pounds)	*2 tablespoons butter, melted*
⅔ cup milk	*½ teaspoon cinnamon*
⅓ cup sugar	*⅛ teaspoon lemon extract*
Marshmallows for topping (optional)	

Cook the sweet potatoes in water to cover, gently boiling until tender, about 25 minutes. Remove skins and mash potatoes in a deep bowl. Add the milk, sugar, egg, butter, cinnamon and lemon extract. Beat until creamy. Grease a 6-cup baking dish with butter, fill it with the sweet potato mixture. Bake in a preheated 350-degree oven for 45 minutes or until firm in the center.

If you wish to add the marshmallow topping, take the baking dish out of the oven after 35 minutes. Place the marshmallows on top. Put it back in the oven for 10 minutes; the topping will brown and puff up. *Serves 5.*

Mexican Refried Beans
(*Frijoles Refritos*)

LET THE MARIACHIS play for the goodness of refried beans.
Eat this dish with a fried egg for breakfast or lunch. Serve
it as a side dish for supper. Refried beans are eaten with
tostados, which are fried tortillas — the bread of Mexico.

2 cups canned pinto beans	*1 small green chili,*
½ small onion, cut up fine	*cut up fine*
2 tablespoons salad oil	*Salt to taste*

Wash the canned beans, drain them. Mash the beans on
a plate, put them in a bowl, and stir in 3 tablespoons water.

In a saucepan, sauté (fry) the onion in the oil until
golden, stirring constantly with a spoon. Add the mashed
beans, mix thoroughly. Stir in the chili and salt. Cook over
low heat for 5 minutes, stirring constantly, making a smooth
dry paste. May be served with wedges of cheddar cheese
stuck into the refried beans, with shredded lettuce and
a few radishes on the side. *Serves 3.*

Fish Caribbean

FISHERMEN bring in their catch every day from the clear waters of the Caribbean. In the palm-sheltered villages fish is cooked in a rich and spicy tomato sauce, reminding one of an African past.

1 to 1½ pounds red snapper,
   bluefish, or any whole fish
½ lemon
1½ tablespoons butter
1 medium onion, chopped
⅛ teaspoon red pepper

1½ cups chopped tomatoes
   (canned or fresh)
Chopped parsley or
   celery leaves
Salt and pepper to taste·
½ teaspoon salad oil

Have the fish cleaned, the head removed. Wash the fish in cold running water, pat it dry and slice it. Squeeze a little lemon juice over both sides of the fish.

Melt the butter in a sturdy pot over medium heat. Sauté the onion until tender. Add the red pepper and cook one minute longer. Stir in the tomatoes, parsley or celery leaves, salt and pepper. Simmer for 5 minutes. Place the pieces of fish in the tomato sauce. Sprinkle with the salad oil. Simmer gently for 15 minutes.

Serve with boiled rice and spoon the fish-tomato gravy over the rice. *Serves 3 to 4.*

West Indies Molded Rice Pudding

THE ELEGANCE of old France is in this molded rice pudding. The early settlers brought their French tastes and French ways to this tropical setting, adding splendidly to the cooking styles of the West Indies.

½ cup rice	⅛ teaspoon salt
2½ cups water	1 egg
¾ cup evaporated milk	Canned (or cooked)
⅓ cup sugar	sliced peaches with
½ teaspoon vanilla	syrup
1/16 teaspoon nutmeg	

Wash the rice in a strainer under cold running water. Bring 2½ cups water to a boil in a saucepan. Stir in the rice, simmer over low heat for 20 minutes until the rice is cooked and the water is absorbed. Remove from heat and add the milk, sugar, vanilla, nutmeg and salt. Stir with a wooden spoon and cook over medium heat for 3 minutes. Then cook over low heat, stirring constantly, for 15 minutes until the rice holds together in a thick mass. Remove from heat.

When the rice has cooled, but still has heat in it, beat the egg with an egg beater. Stir the egg into the rice, mixing thoroughly. Rinse a rounded dish or mold in cold water. Pack the rice into it. Refrigerate at least 6 hours.

To unmold, place the dish in warm-to-hot water for ½ minute, put a plate over the top and turn over. Serve with the peaches around the mold and spoon the peach syrup over the rice. *Serves 4.*

Puerto Rican Little Butter Cookies
(*Mantecaditos*)

THE OLDEST to the youngest enjoy the happy family get-together on Sundays in Puerto Rico. Someone plays a guitar while others sing. And the little butter cookies, made by the dozens, quickly disappear.

4 tablespoons butter	*½ teaspoon almond extract*
4 tablespoons solid	*1¼ cups flour*
shortening	*3 maraschino cherries,*
4 tablespoons sugar	*cut into eighths*

Beat the butter and shortening until smooth in a deep bowl. Add the sugar, mix well. Add the almond extract. Sift the flour, stir it into the butter mixture until the mixture holds together. Do not overmix.

Taking up the mixture with a teaspoon, form into little balls the size of a walnut. Place on an ungreased cookie sheet and flatten with your fingers. Press a cherry sliver into the center. Bake in a preheated 350-degree oven for 25 minutes or until delicately browned. *Makes 23 cookies.*

Colombian Fruit Salad
(*Ensalada de Fruta*)

BANANAS from the tropical lowlands along the Caribbean are mixed with the luscious fruits from the highlands of the Andes. Made into a refreshing dessert of delicate flavors, it is enough to make the Colombians poetic.

1 ripe banana, sliced
1/4 cantaloupe, cubed
1 pear or 1/2 apple,
   peeled and diced

3/4 cup milk or cream,
   mixed with
   1 teaspoon sugar
Cinnamon

Put the banana, cantaloupe, and pear or apple into a deep bowl. Pour the milk or cream over the fruit, keeping the banana deep in the milk so that it will not turn brown. Refrigerate. When ready to serve, spoon fruit salad into individual bowls and dust each serving with cinnamon. *Serves 4.*

Peruvian Pie of the Sierra
(*Pastel de la Sierra*)

HIGH in the mountains of Peru, the potato has been culti-
vated since ancient times by the Incas. Today in the lively
marketplace you can see potatoes of many varieties and
colors. Pie of the Sierra is an elegant potato dish, an example
of the highly developed art of cooking of Peru.

3 large potatoes, cooked,	*6 to 8 ounces cheddar*
peeled and sliced	*cheese, sliced thin*
(1½ pounds)	*2 egg whites*
2 medium tomatoes	*2 egg yolks*
3 tablespoons salad oil	*2 tablespoons cream*
1 large onion, chopped fine	*⅛ teaspoon salt*
1 clove garlic, minced	

To cook the potatoes, place them in a large saucepan with
water to cover. Bring to a boil, then cook over high heat for
30 minutes or until tender. Test with a fork.

Grate the tomatoes, making at least ¾ cup. Heat the
oil until it is hot in a saucepan. Add the onion and garlic,
sauté until tender. Add the tomatoes, simmer over low
heat for 8 minutes.

Grease the bottom and sides of an 8-by-8-inch baking dish.
Using half of the potatoes, cover the bottom of the dish.
Spoon half of the tomato sauce over the potatoes, place
half of the cheese slices on the sauce.

Make another layer with the remaining potatoes. Spoon

the tomato sauce over the potatoes, arrange the cheese slices on top.

Beat the egg whites (add a pinch of salt) until foamy. Mix the egg yolks, cream and salt. Fold the egg whites into the yolk mixture and spoon it over the cheese layer. Bake in a preheated 350-degree oven for 1 hour or until golden brown. *Serves 6.*

Chilean Humitas

THE INDIANS of Chile have put corn leaves to good use in their cooking. Used to enclose foods, the foods are nicely cooked in these excellent leaf wrappings. Humitas, a favorite food in Chile, are made by the potful.

2 ears corn	*2 tablespoons chopped onion*
2 teaspoons solid	*⅛ teaspoon salt*
shortening	*⅛ teaspoon chili powder*

Strip the ears of corn. Discard the silk and dark outer leaves. Save all other leaves for wrapping. Grate the corn ears on a grater and scrape the milk from the cob with a spoon; this equals about ¾ cup.

Heat the shortening in a saucepan. Sauté the onion until tender. Add the salt, chili powder and grated corn.

Stir with a wooden spoon and cook over low heat for 8 to 10 minutes until thick.

Wash the corn leaves; wipe them dry. Using 2 leaves for each wrapping, cut them to measure 6 inches, cutting away points and tough bottom ends. Place narrow leaf ends one on the other, covering 3 inches. Place 2 tablespoons of corn mixture in the center as shown (sketch 1). Tuck in the sides (sketch 2). Bring the inner leaf over the filling and around the sides, enclosing the filling (sketch 3). Then bring the outer leaf over and around the sides. Tie packet tightly with strips torn from tender corn leaves (sketch 4).

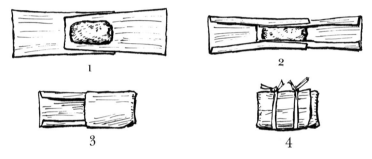

Cook the humitas in salted boiling water (6 cups water and ½ teaspoon salt) for 30 minutes. Each person unwraps the humitas in his plate and eats the filling with a fork. *Makes 4 humitas.*

Argentinean Apple Pancake
(*Panqueque de Manzana*)

IN BUENOS AIRES the apple pancake with a crunchy caramelized topping deserves an "abrazo," a hug and a pat on the back. Or maybe a bouquet of flowers bought from the flower vendors that dot so many corners of the city.

1 egg, beaten	*2½ tablespoons milk*
1 tablespoon flour	*1½ tablespoons butter*
¹⁄₁₆ teaspoon salt	*½ apple, sliced thin*

Sugar for caramelizing

Mix the egg, flour, salt and milk into a smooth batter. Melt the butter in a 6- or 7-inch skillet, swirl it to cover bottom and sides. Sauté the apple slices over medium heat until tender and browned on both sides. Pour in the batter. Cook over low heat. Lift the edges, allowing uncooked part to run under and the batter to set.

To turn the pancake over, slip it onto a plate, then slip the uncooked side back into the skillet. Almost immediately, slip pancake onto the plate again. Melt a heaping tablespoon of sugar in the skillet; it will brown quickly. Slip the well-done side of the pancake onto the syrup. Cook for 1 minute, juggling the skillet. Serve the pancake caramelized side up. *Serves 2.*

Uruguayan Grilled Steak
(*Biftec a la Parrilla*)

IN THE CITY STREETS and along the many beach resorts of Uruguay, a familiar smell seems to permeate the air — meat on the grill. Or parrillada, as it is called. The Uruguayan family goes to the restaurant where enormous strips of meat are grilled and the atmosphere is alive with good humor.

1 pound boneless sirloin,   *1 clove garlic, sliced*
flank steak or chuck steak;   *Salt and pepper*
1 to 1½ inches thick

Cut little slits in the steak, insert the garlic slices. Season with salt and pepper. Place the steak on a shallow pan. Preheat the broiler at high heat, broil the steak 3 to 4 inches from the heat for 8 to 10 minutes or until it is crisp along the edges and redness disappears. Turn, and broil the other side until browned but still juicy. Serve sizzling hot. *Serves 3.*

Uruguayan Gaucho Torta Frita

TORTA FRITA is the bread of the gauchos, the cowboys of Uruguay. Rugged individuals, they find simple pleasure (especially when it rains) in making torta frita. With it they sip maté (a South American tea) through long silver straws.

1 cup flour, less	*⅛ teaspoon salt*
1 tablespoon	*1 tablespoon butter*
1 teaspoon baking powder	*5 tablespoons water*
6 tablespoons solid shortening for frying	

Mix the flour, baking powder and salt. Mix in the butter with a fork, making a crumbly mixture. Stir in the water. Knead the dough hard on a floured surface for 15 minutes.

Divide the dough in half and roll into balls. Flatten a ball of dough. Lift it up and from the top pull the dough

out along the edges, pressing with your thumbs, turning the dough, stretching it into a 5-inch circle. Make a tiny hole through the center with your index finger. Prepare the second ball of dough.

Melt the shortening in a medium-sized saucepan. When hot but not smoking, fry the circles of dough one at a time over medium heat until golden brown (they will puff up), turning once if necessary. Drain on absorbent paper. *Makes 2 tortas fritas.*

Brazilian Rice
(*Arroz*)

EVERYTHING is overwhelming in Brazil; the size of the country, the winding roads through lush tropical mountains, the friendliness of the people. You might even be overwhelmed by the taste of rice, cooked Brazilian style.

1 tablespoon salad oil
½ small onion, chopped
1 clove garlic, crushed
1 tablespoon chopped parsley
  or celery leaves

½ cup rice
1⅓ cups boiling water
¼ teaspoon salt

Heat the oil in a medium-sized saucepan. Add the onion, garlic and parsley. Cook and stir over medium heat until onion is golden. Add the rice, stirring constantly over low heat for 3 minutes. Carefully add the boiling water at once — the rice will "jump." Stir, add the salt and stir again. Cover, simmer gently for 15 minutes or until the rice is cooked and the water is absorbed. Keep covered until ready to serve. *Serves 3.*

Brazilian Coconut Candy
(*Cocadas*)

FOR CANDY rich and sweet, the Brazilians look for their favorite "Bahiana" in the busy shopping areas. Dressed in her colorful costume, she sits behind her candies and cakes — a display of marvelous temptations.

> *1 cup sugar*
> *¼ cup water*
> *1 cup shredded coconut*

Mix the sugar and water in a saucepan. Cook over medium heat, stirring constantly, to a soft-ball stage. (To test it, drop a little syrup into a cup of cold water; it should drop as a thread and dissolve as it reaches bottom.) Remove from heat. Beat for ½ minute, add the coconut and beat for another ½ minute. Now quickly pick up a little of the mixture with the stirring spoon, scoop it off with a teaspoon onto a large plate. Allow to cool. *Makes 12 cocadas.*

Brazilian Fudge Balls
(*Brigadeiro*)

1 15-ounce can sweetened condensed milk (1½ cups)
3 tablespoons cocoa
1 tablespoon butter
For rolling: chocolate shot (or jimmies), chopped nuts, powdered sugar or fine bread crumbs

Cook the milk, cocoa and butter in a saucepan over low heat for 10 minutes (stirring constantly with a wooden spoon) until the mixture thickens and sticks together in a mass. Remove from heat. Empty contents onto a plate and allow to cool; this takes about 35 minutes.

Grease your hands with butter. Pick up a teaspoonful of the mixture, scoop it off with another teaspoon, drop it into your palm and roll it lightly into a ball. Dip it into any of the rolling ingredients. Place it on a large plate, arranging the balls nicely as you make them. *Makes 25 balls of brigadeiro.*

Canadian Popovers

LET's pop over to Canada for some popovers. Popovers are good; they puff up and swell out, being all crispy crust and no crumb. Break them open while they are hot and butter them.

2 eggs	*1 cup flour*
1 cup milk	*½ teaspoon salt*

Grease an 8-cup muffin pan (with butter or shortening) generously, or the batter will stick to the pan. Be sure the rims at the top are well greased. Place the muffin pan in a preheated 450-degree oven while you make the batter.

In a mixing bowl beat the eggs, milk, flour and salt with a rotary beater until well blended. Very carefully and with the use of potholders take the hot muffin pan out of the oven. Spoon the liquid batter into the cups one-half full. Bake in the 450-degree oven for 15 minutes, then lower the heat to 350 degrees and bake 15 to 20 minutes or until well browned. *Makes 8 popovers.*

Canadian Fish Chowder

FISH, fresh from the ocean, is enthusiastically cooked in a large heavy pot and made into a chowder. In Canada, that's what the fishermen have been doing for years. It's a satisfying all-year-round dish.

2 large potatoes, cubed	*1 medium onion,*
1 carrot, diced	*chopped*
2 cups water	*1 cup water*
1 teaspoon salt	*¼ teaspoon salt*
Freshly ground black pepper	*2 cups milk*
1 pound haddock or cod	*Butter*

Put the potatoes, carrot, water, salt and a grind or two of pepper in a saucepan. Bring to a boil, then simmer gently over low heat for 20 minutes until vegetables are cooked.

Meanwhile, wash the fish, cut it into pieces. Put it in a separate saucepan with the onion, water and salt. Cook gently for 20 minutes. Remove the bones, add the fish and fish soup to the cooked vegetables. Stir, pour in the milk, cook until hot, but do not boil. Add a chunk of butter and serve. *Serves 4.*

English Tea Sandwiches

THE BREAK for tea in the late afternoon is traditional in England. Tasty little sandwiches "keep you going" until dinner time. And a serving of a rich pastry or dessert puts you in a wonderful mood.

Bread, white or brown, thinly sliced, crusts removed
Butter, beaten soft and creamy

FILLINGS FOR SANDWICHES

CUCUMBER

½ cucumber, thinly sliced
Salt and pepper

Butter the bread, top with cucumber slices, and season with salt and pepper to taste.

EGG

1 egg, hard-cooked (see Liver Spread)
Mayonnaise
Salt and pepper

Mash the egg and mix with mayonnaise to moisten, salt and pepper to taste. Spread on buttered bread.

BANANA

1 ripe banana
½ teaspoon lemon juice

Mash the banana. Mix in the lemon juice. Spread on bread. *Makes 4 to 6 sandwiches of each variety.*

Irish Buttermilk Oaten Bread

THE LILT of Irish laughter must come from the good home-
made Irish bread that goes so well with a cup of hot tea.
This repast is one of the pleasures from Blarney Castle to
the Highlands of Donegal, and back again.

1½ cups fine oatmeal
1½ cups buttermilk or sour milk
(to make sour milk, see New England Sour Milk Pie)

1¾ cups flour   *1 teaspoon salt*
1½ teaspoons baking soda   *1½ tablespoons sugar*

If you use "old-fashioned" oatmeal, crush the oatmeal in
your hands to refine it. The day before making bread, mix

the oatmeal with the buttermilk or sour milk in a bowl. Cover; let stand overnight.

To make the bread, sift the flour, baking soda, salt and sugar into a deep mixing bowl. Stir in the oatmeal mixture, knead it with your hand, making a soft ball of dough. Dust with flour if the dough is sticky.

On a lightly floured surface roll out the dough into a round loaf 1½ inches thick and 6½ inches across. Give it a nice round shape by cupping it with your hands. Now cut the loaf into quarters, using a floured butter knife. Cut all the way through, but do not separate the sections.

Place on a lightly floured baking tray. Bake in a preheated 350-degree oven for 55 minutes or until well browned.

For a special treat, mix ½ cup raisins (plumped in hot water and patted dry) into the dough just before shaping the loaf. *Makes 1 loaf.*

A Norwegian Sunday Breakfast
(Søndags Frokost)

IN NORWAY this is a special-occasion breakfast for family and friends. Foods are arranged on a table and each person conveniently helps himself. Serve any or as many varieties of herring, cheese and bread as you wish. Then listen to the ohs and ahs of satisfaction.

SOFT-BOILED EGGS

Cook eggs in gently boiling water for 3½ to 4½ minutes. Keep warm and covered in a cotton-napkin-lined basket. Eggs are eaten from the shell in egg cups.

PICKLED HERRING

Use varieties that come in cans or jars: herring in wine sauce, or in sour cream, or dill-flavored herring. Serve sardines with chopped raw onion on the side.

CHEESE

Cheddar-type cheeses, Caraway, Edam or Swiss, sliced.

BREAD

Good solid white and dark breads, thinly sliced.
Ry-Krisp wafers and crackers. And butter.

TOMATOES AND CUCUMBERS

Sliced and arranged on same dish.

COOKED OATMEAL

STEWED PRUNES

Serve hot from a deep serving bowl.

MILK IN LARGE GLASSES. HOT COFFEE FOR GROWN-UPS.

Swedish Prune Pudding

(*Svaskon Cram*)

THE SMORGASBORD in Sweden is a table full of good food. Appetizers, salads, cold and hot dishes, and desserts are on display to tempt you. Let prune pudding be your temptation.

½ *pound prunes*
    (about 22 prunes)
2½ *cups water*
3 *tablespoons sugar*
2½ *teaspoons lemon juice*

½ *teaspoon cinnamon*
2 *teaspoons potato*
    starch (or 1 table-
    spoon flour)

Cook the prunes and water in a saucepan over medium heat for 35 minutes until prunes are tender. Remove prunes to a plate, allow to cool. Remove pits. Measure prune liquid. Add water, if necessary, to make 1 cup.

Put liquid and prunes back into saucepan. Stir in the sugar, lemon juice, cinnamon and potato starch. Cook over medium heat, stirring constantly, until thickened. Do not overcook.

Turn into a serving dish. Allow to cool, then chill. Serve topped with whipped cream. *Serves 4.*

35

Finnish Parish House Emergency—
A Bread Pudding
(*Pappilan Hätävara*)

HOSPITALITY is never overlooked in Finland. Even the dessert "Parish House Emergency" is so named to take care of guests who stop in unexpectedly. Someone wants to please you and does, with individual bread puddings.

6 slices wholewheat bread,	*4 teaspoons sugar*
or good solid white bread	*¼ teaspoon salt*
2 eggs, beaten	*Jam*
1⅓ cups milk	*Whipped cream*

Tear the bread into 1-inch pieces. Mix the eggs, milk, sugar and salt in a bowl. Soak bread in the milk mixture.

Butter 4 custard cups. Spoon a layer of bread to cover the bottom of each, spread lightly with the jam. Add another layer of bread, spread again with jam, and top with bread. Spoon any remaining liquid around the sides. Bake in a preheated 350-degree oven for 40 minutes or until the top is crispy and brown. Serve warm, topped with whipped cream. *Serves 4.*

Danish Hamburger
(*Hakkeboef*)

HAMBURGER lovers of the world, unite and come to Denmark! In this land of rich and beautiful farms there are eggs, butter, cheese and meats. And a wonderful way of serving hamburgers with soft-fried onions.

½ pound ground beef	*Flour*
1 tablespoon chopped onion	*1 tablespoon butter or*
Salt and pepper	*margarine*

SOFT-FRIED ONION

½ tablespoon butter or	*2 tablespoons water*
margarine	*Salt and sugar*
½ small onion, sliced	

Mix the beef and onion. Sprinkle with a little salt and pepper. Mix and divide in half. Shape into thick 4½-inch hamburgers, then dip lightly in flour. Heat the butter in a skillet. Over medium to high heat fry the hamburgers, 4 to 5 minutes on each side.

In another skillet melt the butter. Sauté the onion over medium heat until golden brown. Add the water (it will sizzle) and over low heat allow the water to evaporate. Sprinkle with salt and sugar, cook ½ minute. Serve the soft-fried onion over the hamburgers. *Serves 2.*

The Netherlands—
Tomato Soup with Meatballs
(*Tomatensoep met Balletjes*)

HERE is a soup that is a real Dutch treat. But don't leave the table yet! This is just the beginning of a meal, for the people of the Netherlands like to eat abundantly and well.

1 onion, chopped	*Beef bone*
1 stalk celery with leaves, sliced	*6 cups water*
1 carrot, diced	*½ teaspoon salt*
2 cups tomatoes, canned	
or fresh	

Bring onion, celery, carrot, tomatoes, beef bone, water and salt to a boil in a large saucepan. Then simmer over low heat 1½ hours or until vegetables and any meat on the bone are cooked. Remove the bone, put the soup through a strainer, mashing the vegetables with a fork. Put the soup and mashed vegetables back into the saucepan, add 2 cups water and salt to taste.

½ pound ground beef	*2 teaspoons bread crumbs*
1 small egg, beaten	

Mix the beef, egg and bread crumbs. Form into ½-inch meatballs, making about 36. Bring the soup to a boil, turn to medium heat, then drop the meatballs gently into the soup and cook for 10 minutes. Each person gets 6 to 7 meatballs in the soup. *Serves 5.*

38

French Dessert Crêpes

THE GOOD COOK in France keeps a special frying pan for omelets and crêpes. The pan is never washed; it is wiped clean. For dessert crêpes, the paper-thin pancakes can be made ahead of time, then rolled and prepared for broiling just before serving.

1 egg	*¼ cup milk*
½ cup flour	*⅓ cup water*
¼ teaspoon salt	*Butter or margarine*
2 teaspoons sugar	

Beat the egg. Mix in the flour, salt, milk and water, making a smooth batter.

Grease a 6-inch skillet lightly with butter or margarine. Over medium to high heat pour 2 tablespoons of the batter into the skillet, tilting it quickly to cover the bottom. When the edges begin to curl, turn the crêpe over, and immediately turn it onto a large plate. Grease the skillet again, make another crêpe; continue until all of the batter is used.

Roll up each crêpe and place them close together in a shallow baking tray. Sprinkle with sugar, broil under high heat for 10 to 12 minutes. Or cook in a preheated 375-degree oven until brown and crispy. *Makes 8 crêpes.*

German Meat Dumplings
(*Fleischklösse*)

THE VARIETIES of sausage and dumplings in Germany are endless. Meats are minced into a fine paste and expertly flavored with spices and herbs. For sausage, the mixture is stuffed into sausage skins, while dumplings are rolled into balls and poached in salted boiling water.

3½ tablespoons margarine	*A grind of black pepper*
1 egg	*Pinch of nutmeg (optional)*
⅓ cup cooked meat or	*1 cup dry bread crumbs*
chicken, finely chopped	

In a mixing bowl whip the margarine until creamy. Beat in the egg. Add the meat, pepper, nutmeg and bread crumbs. Stir, then knead the mixture with your hand. Roll into 6 balls for dumplings.

Bring 6 cups water and 1 teaspoon salt to a boil. Drop dumplings into the water, simmer over medium heat for 10 minutes. Drain. Dumplings may be served with sauerkraut, spinach or any gravy. They can also be cooked and served in a soup. *Serves 3.*

Polish Salad
(*Salata*)

AFTER a long cold winter and a limited diet of potatoes, cabbage and buckwheat groats, the Polish housewife is delighted when spring comes and freshly grown vegetables can be made into a salad.

¼ head lettuce
1 tomato, cut into wedges

½ small onion,
sliced paper thin
Mayonnaise

Wash the lettuce, drain and cut into chunks. Put the lettuce, tomato and onion in a deep bowl and mix gently with a heaping tablespoon mayonnaise. Serve immediately or refrigerate for later use. The mayonnaise mixed with the juice of the tomato makes a special taste, delicate and refreshing. *Serves 2.*

Russian Noodle Kigel

(*Lukshena Kügel*)

ALL SMILES. That's what you will see in the Ukraine, the wheatlands of Russia, where Granny knows how to keep everyone happy with the noodle kigel that she makes, and a glass of hot tea flavored with jam or a slice of apple.

½ pound medium noodles (about 4 cups)
4 tablespoons margarine
3 eggs, beaten

1¼ teaspoons salt
½ pound cottage cheese (about 1 cup)
2 tablespoons margarine

Cook the noodles in boiling salted water (8 cups water and 1 teaspoon salt) for 10 minutes until tender. Remove from heat, add a little water from the tap and drain. Stir in the margarine, eggs, salt and cottage cheese.

Melt the 2 tablespoons margarine in an 8-by-8-inch baking dish. Grease the bottom and sides. Heat the dish ½ minute over low heat. Pour in the noodle mixture, filling the corners well. Bake in a preheated 375-degree oven for 50 minutes or until golden brown on top. *Serves 6.*

Czechoslovakian Fruit Dumplings
(*Ovocné Knedlíky*)

THANK YOU, Czechoslovakia, for fruit dumplings. Served after a soup, they are a combination of main dish and dessert. Fruits in season are wrapped in a dough, four to six dumplings to a serving.

Plums, apricots,	*1 cup flour*
strawberries, cherries	*2 tablespoons milk*
or blueberries	*Sugar*
1 egg	*Grated cheese (optional)*
4 tablespoons cream cheese	*Melted butter*

Wash the fruit, pat it dry. Remove pits or seeds. Cut large plums and apricots in half; use a cluster of strawberries, cherries or blueberries for filling.

To make the dough wrapping, beat the egg, beat in the cream cheese until smooth. Stir in the flour and milk. Knead lightly, dusting with flour for easier handling. Roll out half the dough at a time on a lightly floured surface, to just under 1/4-inch thick. Cut into 2 1/2-inch squares.

Place fruit in the center of each square, sprinkle with sugar if fruit is tart. Bring the corners together at the top, pinch the sides closed and roll into a ball.

Bring 6 cups water and 1 teaspoon salt to a boil. Drop the dumplings into the water, cook for 10 minutes, drain.

Sprinkle each serving with sugar, grated cheese and melted butter. *Makes 16 to 18 dumplings.*

Yugoslavian Meat Stew
(*Djuveć*)

YUGOSLAVIA, a wildly rugged and beautiful country, is in many areas still untouched by modern ways. In the mountain villages hospitality is offered to the traveler. It might be djuveć, a highly flavorful stew, or a dish of preserves (eaten by the spoonful) and a glass of cold water.

1 can tomatoes (2-cup size)	*2 medium onions, chopped*
1½ tablespoons margarine	*⅓ cup rice*
	½ teaspoon salt
1 pound shoulder of lamb, cut into 2-inch pieces	*¼ teaspoon pepper*
	1 green pepper, sliced

Separate the tomatoes from tomato liquid. Put some tomatoes aside for topping. Pour tomato liquid into a measuring cup, add water to make 1 cup.

Melt the margarine in a large saucepan. Add the meat, brown on all sides. Push meat to the side of the saucepan, add the onions and cook 5 minutes. Remove saucepan from heat, stir in the rice, salt, pepper, tomatoes and tomato liquid. Pour mixture into a 2-quart baking dish, add tomato topping. Cover and bake in a preheated 375-degree oven for 1 hour or until rice is tender. *Serves 4.*

Greek Lentil Soup
(*Fahkee*)

IN A REMOTE mountain village or along the seafront of
Greece, a man can be happy today as in ancient times, with
a bowl of lentil soup and a dish of olives. Know the pleasures
of eating lentils, the dried little seeds of the pea family.

¾ cup lentils	*½ cup tomato sauce*
3½ cups water	*½ teaspoon salt*
2 cloves garlic, unpeeled	*2½ tablespoons olive oil*

Empty the lentils into a dish. Look them over, remove
any gravel. Put the lentils into a saucepan, rinse with cold
running water and drain.

Add the 3½ cups water and garlic. Bring to a boil. Turn
to low heat, stir in the tomato sauce, salt and olive oil.
Simmer gently for 50 minutes. Add water if the soup becomes too thick, stir and bring to a boil. *Serves 3.*

Italian Spaghetti with Garlic and Oil
(*Spaghetti al Aglio e Olio*)

IT WOULD NOT BE southern Italy without garlic and olive oil. There should be a festival honoring these two foods (and garlands of garlic to dance with) for the beautiful way they flavor a dish of spaghetti.

¼ *pound thin spaghetti*	*Salt*
3 to 4 cloves garlic	*Freshly ground black pepper*
3 tablespoons olive oil	*Chopped parsley or basil*

Cook the spaghetti in rapidly boiling water (6 cups water and 1 teaspoon salt) for 10 to 12 minutes. Spaghetti should be tender but firm, *al dente,* as the Italians call it.

Meanwhile, crush the garlic by putting it between a folded-over piece of waxed paper and mashing it with a hammer. Heat the oil in a saucepan. Add the garlic, stir, cook over low heat for 3 minutes or until garlic is golden.

Drain the spaghetti. Empty it into the saucepan with the oil and garlic. Stir, add salt to taste and a few grinds of pepper. Mix well. Serve hot in a deep dish, sprinkle generously with parsley or basil. *Serves 2.*

Spain—Galician Tuna Salad
(*Ensalada de Atún*)

THE GALICIANS say their fjord-like coast (in the northwest corner of Spain) was created to look like the fingers of a hand. What good fish comes from this rugged area of mountains and sea, where tuna salad is an appetizer!

1 7-ounce can tuna	*2 to 3 radishes, sliced*
2 cooked potatoes,	*1½ tablespoons olive oil*
peeled and diced (see	*2½ tablespoons lemon*
Peruvian Pie of the Sierra)	*juice*
½ cup sliced cooked beets	*Salt and pepper*

In a large bowl, break the tuna into chunks. Add the potatoes, beets and radishes. Toss gently. Mix in the oil and lemon juice. Season with salt and pepper to taste. *Serves 4 to 6.*

48

Spain—Seville Bread Puffs
(*Torrejas*)

IF THE ANDALUSIAN sings, could it be because of torrejas? In Seville these lovely little bread puffs are flavored with orange and scented with cinnamon. Nice to have around when company comes, to serve with milk, coffee or tea.

3 slices good white
bread, cut in half
1 egg, well beaten with
a dash of salt

¾ cup milk
Orange juice
Cinnamon

Grease generously with margarine the bottom and sides of an 8-by-8-inch baking dish. Dip the bread in the milk, place the bread to the side of the bowl to drain, then dip it into the beaten egg, coating both sides.

Arrange bread in the baking dish. Bake in a preheated 375-degree oven for 40 minutes or until crisp and brown.

To serve, sprinkle torrejas with orange juice, dust lightly with cinnamon. Or if you prefer, dust with a mixture of cinnamon and sugar. *Serves 3.*

Moroccan Cocoa Cookies

(*Biscuits au Caboel*)

WHAT SMELLS so good in the Casbah? It's the food. Exquisite use is made of spices and herbs. Glasses of mint tea come at the end of a meal with trays of cookies and pastries.

2 cups flour	*½ cup sugar*
½ teaspoon baking powder	*⅓ cup salad oil*
⅛ teaspoon salt	*2 tablespoons cocoa*
2 eggs	*1½ tablespoons water*

Sift the flour, baking powder and salt. In a deep bowl mix the eggs, beat in the sugar and oil. Add the flour mixture, knead with your hand. Mix the cocoa and water in a cup. Divide dough in half, add cocoa mixture to one half, mixing thoroughly.

On a lightly floured surface roll out plain dough to measure 7 by 14 inches and 1/4-inch thick. Roll out cocoa

dough to the same size, place it over the plain dough, press together with the rolling pin. Roll up dough lengthwise, cut into 1/4-inch slices and place on a baking sheet. Bake in a preheated 350-degree oven for 20 to 25 minutes. *Makes 32 cookies.*

Mozambique Chum-Chum

CHUM-CHUM (meaning hot-hot) is made for special occasions. In Mozambique, friends help with the building of a house and the host provides chum-chum, little crunchy meatballs to pop in the mouth.

¼ *pound ground beef*	¼ *teaspoon salt*
½ *small onion, finely chopped*	*Dash of black pepper*
1 strip green pepper, minced	⅛ *teaspoon red pepper*

Mix the beef, onion, green pepper, salt, black pepper and red pepper. Divide in half, then divide each half into 8 balls, making 16 meatballs.

DOUGH WRAPPING

⅔ *cup flour*	*1 small egg, well beaten*
¼ *cup cornmeal*	*2 tablespoons water*
¼ *teaspoon salt*	½ *cup salad oil for*
1 tablespoon solid	*deep frying*
shortening	

Mix the flour, cornmeal and salt in a bowl. Mix in the shortening with a fork, making a crumbly mixture. Stir in the egg, add the water and knead to a pliable dough. Divide the dough in half, divide each half into 8 balls, making 16 balls of dough. Flatten the dough, stretching it into 3-inch circles. Place a meatball in the center of each circle, wrap the dough around it, pinching the edges closed. Roll gently into a ball.

Heat the oil in a saucepan. Fry the chum-chum over medium heat, one at a time, until golden brown. Remove with a large slotted spoon and drain on absorbent paper. *Makes 16 chum-chum.*

Kenyan Chicken and Bread
(*Kuku Na Ugli*)

THE ARAB and Indian traders brought spices to the east coast of Africa. And the Kenyans used the spices with a light and knowing touch, creating highly flavorful foods. Some of the good cooking of the Caribbean and Brazil originated here.

1 medium onion, chopped	*2 tomatoes, cubed*
1 tablespoon margarine	*¼ teaspoon salt*
½ 3-pound frying	*½ teaspoon curry powder*
chicken, cut into	*⅛ teaspoon red pepper*
serving pieces	*⅓ cup water*

In a saucepan sauté the onion in the margarine over medium heat for 3 minutes. Add the chicken and brown it on all sides. Add the tomatoes, salt, curry powder, red pepper and water. Bring to a boil, turn to low heat and simmer, covered, for 30 minutes, or until chicken is tender.

BREAD

⅔ cup water	*⅓ cup cornmeal, mixed with*
	⅓ cup water

To make the bread, boil the water in a saucepan. Stir in the cornmeal mixture. Cook over medium heat for 5 minutes or until thickened. Spread the cornmeal on a large plate. Cut the bread into pieces or tear it by hand. And use it for dipping into the chicken gravy. *Serves 3.*

Saudi Arabian Basbousa

BASBOUSA is a syrupy sweet and delightfully rich pastry dessert. Perhaps the camel caravans and ancient dhows (Arab ships) brought the love for this sweet to distant lands, and to the many different peoples of the Arab world.

5 tablespoons solid shortening   *1½ cups sugar*
1½ cups farina (Cream of Wheat) *1 cup milk*

In a deep bowl beat the shortening until creamy. Stir in the farina, sugar and milk. Beat until smooth. Cover and leave the mixture in the bowl at room temperature overnight.

To bake the basbousa, grease the bottom and sides of an 8-by-8-inch baking dish. Pour in the mixture and spread it smooth. Bake in a preheated 350-degree oven for 45 minutes or until crisp on top and a rich golden color. Meanwhile, make the syrup.

1 cup sugar   *2 teaspoons lemon juice*
½ cup water

Mix the sugar, water and lemon juice in a saucepan. Bring to a boil, stirring constantly, then simmer gently for 10 minutes, stirring occasionally, until the syrup is slightly thickened. As soon as the basbousa comes out of the oven, cut into about 1½-inch squares, then pour the syrup over it. *Makes 25 squares of basbousa.*

Israeli Eggplant
(*Hatzilim*)

ISRAEL, like so many Mediterranean countries, has glorified the eggplant. Seasoned and spiced, sautéed or stuffed, served hot or cold, it is enough to make you want to dance the hora.

1 small eggplant	*1 large unpeeled ripe*
Salt	*tomato, cubed*
¼ cup olive oil	*⅔ cup water*
1 clove garlic, crushed	*¼ teaspoon salt*
1 large onion, chopped	*A grind of black pepper*

Cut the eggplant into ½-inch slices. Peel the slices, salt them lightly and arrange in a deep dish, one slice on another. Weigh them down with 2 or 3 inverted small plates for 30 minutes, to squeeze liquid from the eggplant.

Rinse the eggplant in cold water and wipe dry, then cut the slices into quarters. Heat the oil in a large skillet. Sauté the garlic and onion for 5 minutes over medium heat. Add the eggplant, tomato, water, salt and pepper. Cook, stirring gently, for 3 minutes. Cover and simmer over low heat for 40 minutes. Serve it as you would any vegetable. It is excellent served cold as an appetizer. *Serves 5.*

Lebanese Squash Omelet
(*Imfarakat Koosa*)

IF YOU have never eaten squash, here is an appealing intro-
duction. When squash omelet is made in a large skillet (just
double the recipe) the Lebanese cut it into small pieces for
appetizers and into wedges for individual servings.

1 6- or 7-inch yellow squash	*1½ tablespoons butter*
2 eggs	*¼ cup chopped onion*
2 tablespoons water	*Salt and pepper*
⅟₁₆ teaspoon salt	

Wash and dry the squash. Trim the ends. Cut squash into
¼-inch slices, then cut slices in half. Beat the eggs, water and
salt in a bowl. Heat the butter in a small skillet. Sauté the
onion over medium heat until soft. Add the squash, cook
over low heat until tender, about 15 minutes. Season lightly
with salt and pepper.

Stir the egg mixture, pour it over the squash. Continue
cooking over low heat. As the eggs become firm around the
edges, lift the edges allowing the uncooked eggs to run
under. When the omelet is almost set, divide it in half,
loosening it from the skillet. The omelet should be slightly
moist. Serve hot or cold. *Serves 2.*

Turkish Bean Flatterer
(*Fasulya Piazi*)

IT SEEMS the food of Turkey is prepared to entice one, to appeal to the taste and to please the eye. Food is arranged on a dish almost lovingly, making each man feel like a Sultan and each lady, a special lady.

1½ cups canned lima beans
or small white beans
½ small onion, sliced
paper thin
Sprig of parsley, chopped
2 tablespoons olive oil

1 tablespoon lemon
juice or vinegar
Salt and pepper to taste
1 hard-cooked egg
(see Liver Spread)
1 medium tomato

Rinse the beans in cold water, drain. Mix beans gently with the onion and parsley. Add the oil, lemon juice or vinegar, salt and pepper. Mix well.

Transfer mixture to a serving dish. Cut egg in half, lengthwise, then cut each half into thirds; they will look like little boats. Arrange egg pieces on the beans. Cut tomato into eighths, place them among the egg pieces. Refrigerate until ready to serve. *Serves 3.*

Armenian Pilaf

THE PEOPLE from the land that was once Armenia have brought their cooking specialties to other parts of the world. Lucky for us! Even the Greeks say, "The Armenians are wonderful cooks."

¾ pound lamb shank
5 cups water
½ teaspoon salt

To make pilaf, the broth must be made first. Put the lamb in a deep pot with the water and salt. Bring to a boil, then simmer over low heat for 1 hour, removing scum from the top. Cool, pour broth into a jar. Refrigerate. Remove fat from the top. When ready to make pilaf, heat the broth.

½ cup rice   *¼ cup fine noodles,*
3 tablespoons margarine   *crushed into small pieces*
1½ cups hot broth

Wash the rice and drain. Heat the margarine in a saucepan over medium heat. Add the noodles, stirring constantly for 2 to 3 minutes until golden brown. Mix in the rice, stir and cook for 3 minutes. Stir in the broth. Simmer, covered, over low heat for 15 minutes or until liquid is absorbed. Remove pot from heat, allowing rice to steam, still covered, for 10 minutes. *Serves 4.*

Afghanistan — Abdul's Kebabs

SHOULD YOU travel in Afghanistan through treacherous mountain passes, over zigzag roads, you will find the trip exhilarating, the passengers friendly. And in Kabul a special treat awaits you — Abdul's Kebabs, grilled over an open fire.

1 cup yogurt or sour cream	*½ teaspoon red pepper*
2 tablespoons catsup	*1¼ pound lamb shoulder*
1 clove garlic, crushed	*or leg, cut into*
1 teaspoon salt	*1½-inch cubes*

In a deep bowl combine the yogurt or sour cream, catsup, garlic, salt and red pepper. Add the lamb, mix well. Refrigerate, covered, overnight or at least 6 hours.

When you are ready to cook, empty lamb mixture into a shallow baking dish. Preheat broiler for 5 minutes at 400 degrees. Broil lamb 4 to 5 inches from the heat until nicely browned on all sides and still juicy (test with a fork). Serve over rice. *Serves 3.*

Tibetan Chapali

IN THE HIGH Himalayas, rooftop of the world, the gracious Tibetans serve endless cups of tea. When chapali, the pastry puffs with meat, are served, you will hear Tibetans say "Shim-bu shitah ray" — it is very delicious.

¼ pound ground beef	*2 teaspoons soy sauce*
1 tablespoon chopped onion	*Garlic salt*

DOUGH WRAPPING

½ cup flour	*3½ tablespoons water*
2 teaspoons solid shortening	*Shortening for frying*

Mix the beef, onion, soy sauce and a sprinkle of garlic salt. Divide into 5 balls. Sift the flour. Add the shortening, cut it into the flour with a fork, making a crumbly mixture. Stir in the water and with your fingers knead all together, dusting lightly if dough is sticky. Divide into 5 balls.

On a lightly floured surface roll dough into 5½-inch circles. Put the meat in the middle, press it down, then gather up dough in the center, enclosing the meat. Be sure there are no openings.

Melt 4 tablespoons shortening in a saucepan. When hot but not smoking, deep-fry the chapali over medium heat until golden brown, pleated side down, then the other side. Drain on absorbent paper. *Makes 5 chapali.*

Indian Upma—A Farina Dish

A DISH for a maharajah! That's what upma is. Spiced just enough to excite the appetite and with a surprising taste of cashew nuts, upma is served in the mornings or anytime between meals.

1 green chili, cut up, or   *12 cashew nuts*
  ⅛ teaspoon red pepper   *⅓ cup salad oil*
1 tablespoon chopped   *2⅓ cups water*
  fresh ginger   *1 teaspoon salt*
½ teaspoon mustard seeds   *1 cup farina (Cream*
⅛ teaspoon cumin   *of Wheat)*

Put the chili (or red pepper), ginger, mustard seeds, cumin and cashew nuts into a small dish.

Heat the oil in a saucepan. Add the ingredients from the dish, stir and cook over low heat for 3 minutes, being sure the nuts do not burn. Add the water, bring to a boil, then stir in the salt.

Turn to low heat and slowly add the farina, stirring constantly, until mixture is smooth and thick. Cover and cook for 5 minutes. Allow to cool. *Serves 4.*

Ceylon Curried Green Beans
(*Bonchi*)

CURRY POWDER is a blend of spices. Each family has its favorite blend, and many like additional hot seasoning. In the beautiful land of Ceylon, the ordinary green bean becomes extraordinary; it's highly spiced, it's curried.

1½ tablespoons salad oil	*⅛ teaspoon paprika*
1 large onion, chopped	*2 teaspoons curry powder*
½ pound green beans,	*Dash of cinnamon*
cut up	*1 cup water*
½ teaspoon salt	*Milk*
¼ teaspoon chili powder	

Heat the oil in a saucepan. Sauté the onion until tender over medium heat. Add the green beans, stir. Add the salt, chili powder, paprika, curry powder, cinnamon and water. Mix well. Bring to a boil, lower heat, cover and cook until green beans are tender and water is absorbed. Add milk, just enough to barely see it, and bring to a boil. Serve at room temperature, with rice and any meat or fish. *Serves 4.*

Chinese Diced Beef and Green Pepper
(*Lak-Ju Now-Yoh Ding*)

IN THE ANCIENT ART of Chinese cooking, the cook prepares steaming delicacies from whatever vegetables are available, adding flavor to the noodle bowls of the North and the rice bowls of the South.

¼ pound beef sirloin	*1 medium onion, slivered*
1 teaspoon soy sauce	*½ green pepper, diced*
½ teaspoon sugar	*Salt*
2 tablespoons salad oil	*1½ teaspoons cornstarch*
1 clove garlic, chopped	*(or 1 teaspoon flour), mixed*
½ cup diced celery	*with ⅓ cup water*

Cut the beef into ½-inch cubes. Combine the soy sauce and sugar. Marinate the beef in this mixture for 15 minutes.

Heat the oil in a large skillet. Fry the garlic for ½ minute. Add the beef, cook quickly over high heat until brown. Push beef to the side of the skillet, add the celery, onion and green pepper. Sprinkle with salt. Cook and stir for 3 minutes; vegetables must be crisp. Add the cornstarch mixture, stir through once. Cover and steam for 1 minute. Remove to a serving dish. Serve with boiled rice. *Serves 2.*

Korean Bulgo-Ki
(*Fired Beef*)

THE KOREANS are glad to have rice and pickled cabbage (kum-chee) everyday and at every meal. They like highly seasoned foods, peppery hot sauces, onions and garlic. Meat is scarce and Bulgo-Ki is a special dish, served on very special occasions.

½ pound beef sirloin, sliced thin, cut across the grain	*⅛ teaspoon garlic powder*
2 tablespoons soy sauce	*Dash of black pepper*
2 teaspoons sugar	*1 green onion, thinly sliced*
	2 teaspoons sesame seeds

Beef that is partially frozen can be cut into thin slices quite easily.

In a bowl mix the soy sauce, sugar, garlic powder, pepper, green onion and sesame seeds. Marinate the beef in this mixture for at least 15 minutes.

When ready to serve, remove the beef from the mixture and broil it under high heat until crisp along the edges. Turn, broil until redness is gone. Serve immediately. *Serves 3.*

66

Japanese Tempura

TEMPURA is a delightful and special dish of Japan. To make it, vegetables are cut imaginatively so that when dipped in batter and deep fried, each texture and subtle flavor can be appreciated.

1 egg	*1 carrot*
3 tablespoons flour	*1 small onion*
⅛ teaspoon salt	*½ cup parsley sprigs*
1 tablespoon water	*½ cup salad oil for deep frying*

To prepare the batter, beat the egg in a bowl. Add the flour, salt and water, and mix until smooth.

Prepare the vegetables. Cut two 2-inch pieces from the carrot, cut in half lengthwise, slice thin, then cut into matchstick pieces. Arrange in clusters, 3 to 4 carrot sticks together.

Cut onion into quarters, then slice into thin wedges.

Remove long stems from the parsley, leaving the leafy clusters together.

Heat the oil in a small saucepan. Once hot, keep over medium heat. (Test with a drop of batter in the oil; batter should brown quickly.) Drop carrot clusters, onion wedges and parsley sprigs one at a time into the batter and with a tablespoon slide them into the deep hot oil. Take out with a fork when golden brown, drain on absorbent paper. Serve with a small dish of soy sauce for dipping. *Serves 3.*

Philippine Chicken Adobo

HERE is a Spanish name for a Filipino dish that has a Chinese flavor. Many exquisite dishes of the Philippines have resulted from years of Spanish rule and close contact with the Chinese.

½ 3-pound frying chicken	1 clove garlic, mashed
2 tablespoons soy sauce	3 or 4 peppercorns
4 tablespoons vinegar	¼ cup water

Cut the chicken into 2-inch pieces, meat and bone together. In a bowl mix the soy sauce, vinegar, garlic and peppercorns. Dip and roll the chicken in the sauce and marinate at least 1 hour.

When ready to cook, put the chicken and the sauce into a saucepan. Cook over medium heat for 5 minutes, turning the chicken on all sides. Add the water, cover and cook over low heat for 25 minutes or until tender. Serve with boiled rice. *Serves 3.*

Australian Pancakes
(*Pikelets*)

IF THE JOLLY Australian wanderer could find Waltzing Matilda and share these pikelets with her, they would surely have something to waltz about. Serve them for breakfast or anytime you feel hunger pangs coming on.

¾ cup flour	*¼ teaspoon salt*
1 tablespoon sugar	*1 egg, beaten*
½ teaspoon baking powder	*½ cup milk*
½ teaspoon baking soda	*Shortening for frying*

Mix the flour, sugar, baking powder, baking soda and salt in a bowl. Mix the egg with the milk and slowly stir it into the flour mixture, making a thick but runny batter.

Heat the shortening (about 2½ tablespoons) in a large skillet; turn to medium heat. Using a tablespoon of batter for each pancake, drop the batter gently onto the skillet, making 2½-inch pancakes. Allow the underside to brown and the top to become bubbly and almost dry. Turn and brown the other side. Serve with jam. *Makes 16 pancakes.*

Index